BIG BOOK OF

BUILDING

Duct Tape, Paper, Cardboard, and Recycled Projects to Blast Away Boredom

by Marne Ventura

CAPSTONE PRESS

a capstone imprint

Table of Contents

Make Amazing Paper Projects! 78

Build Fantastic Recycled Projects! 112

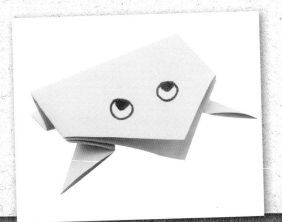

Build Your Imagination!

Have you ever been stuck at home with nothing fun to do? You have the same old games and toys, but you've played with them a million times. You're in luck! You're holding the ultimate cure for boredom. Just find some simple supplies and get ready to make some awesome games and toys, useful stuff, and even cool things you can wear.

Few things are more fun than making cool stuff yourself. Get some big cardboard boxes and turn them into a huge fortress. Build a birdhouse from a coffee can, or make a rubber band-powered car. Create an eerie alien mask or a sci-fi laser sword. You can even turn old boxes into awesome cardboard armor, swords, and shields!

Are you ready to flex your creative muscles? Then dive in and get ready to build some of the coolest stuff you can imagine!

Tips and Tricks

» Get a good cutting mat. Craft stores sell mats with grid lines that help make measuring easy. A wood or plastic cutting board and a ruler will also work well.

» Before starting a project, read through all of the steps and be sure to gather all the necessary materials.

» For large cardboard projects ask people at your local appliance store if they have any big boxes you can use.

Tools Needed

You'll need some common tools to make many of your projects. Gather the following tools and store them in a box so they're easy to find when you need them. Remember to always ask an adult for help when using sharp knives, scissors, or hot glue guns.

scissors	utility knife	hot glue gun	paintbrush
hole punch	cutting board	ruler	yardstick
pliers	paper clamps	rubber bands	saw
 wire cutter	 hammer and nails		

Construct Awesome Cardboard Projects!

What do cereal boxes, shoe boxes, and paper towel tubes all have in common? They're all made from cardboard! Before cardboard was invented, people often used heavy wooden crates for storage and shipping. But when cardboard boxes were created in the 1870s, it was a major step forward for storing and shipping goods. The boxes were strong, lightweight, and cheap.

Today cardboard isn't just used to make boxes. If you look around your home you'll probably find many things made of cardboard. And the great thing about it is you don't have to throw cardboard into the recycling bin. You can use it to make fun projects instead!

Look around for some boxes, tubes, and other cardboard objects. You'll soon be building robots, armor, weapons, and other awesome stuff to impress your friends!

Groovy Guitar

Are you ready for some rock 'n' roll? **Using cardboard, some rubber bands, and a plastic lid, you can make an awesome guitar with a fun, boingy sound. Call a few friends and get ready to rock out!**

MATERIALS

- 5 sheets of corrugated cardboard, 10 by 30 inches (25 by 76 centimeters)
- 3-inch (7.6-cm) wide plastic lid from potato chip container
- 1/8-inch (0.3-cm) wide dowel, 16 inches (41 cm) long
- 4 rubber bands, 7 inches (18 cm) long
- 2 large paper clips
- acrylic paint
- 3 water bottle caps
- drill and 1/8-inch (0.3-cm) drill bit

Step 1: Measure and mark guitar shapes on a sheet of cardboard. The body should measure 10 by 15 inches (25 by 38 cm). The guitar neck should measure 2 by 11 inches (5 by 28 cm). Mark a 3- by 4-inch (7.6- by 10-cm) rectangle on the end of the neck for the guitar head. Cut out the guitar shapes. Use them as patterns to cut out four more body and neck shapes.

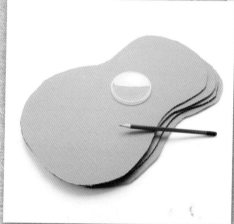

Step 2: Use the lid as a pattern to draw a circle in the center of four guitar body shapes. Cut out the circles.

Step 3: Hot glue the cardboard pieces with holes together. Be sure the sound holes line up with one another. Glue the last body piece that has no hole to the back of the guitar.

Step 4: Paint the front and back of the guitar. Let it dry completely. Add frets to the neck piece with a marker.

Step 5: Measure 1 inch (2.5 cm) from the bottom of the sound hole. Mark a 2.5-inch (6.4-cm) long line at this spot. Measure and mark a 1.5-inch (3.8-cm) long line at the top of the guitar neck. Make a small slit along each line. Place a 2.5-inch (6.4-cm) and a 1.5-inch (3.8-cm) long piece of dowel in the slits and glue them in place.

Step 6: Measure and mark four evenly spaced holes below the sound hole about 0.5 inch (1.3 cm) below the dowel. Measure and mark four more holes about 0.5 inch (1.3 cm) above the dowel in the neck piece. Ask an adult to help you drill 1/8-inch (0.3-cm) wide holes through the guitar at the marks.

Step 7: Snip the rubber bands so they are straight pieces instead of loops. Thread one rubber band through each bottom hole at the back of the guitar. Tie the end of each rubber band to one large paper clip. Turn over the guitar and pull the rubber bands snugly. Thread the other ends of the rubber bands through the top set of holes. Tie the ends to a second paper clip. The paper clips should be snug against the back of the guitar to help hold the rubber bands firmly in place.

Step 8: Cut six 1.5-inch (3.8-cm) long pieces of dowel. Hot glue three of them on each side of the guitar head. Glue key-shaped cardboard cutouts to the ends of the dowels.

Step 9: Glue the three water bottle caps to the lower side of the guitar body for volume and tone control buttons. Now you're ready to rock out!

Tip: Make your guitar look even cooler by painting on lightning bolts or flames.

Model Pirate Ship

Ahoy, mateys! Who needs the high seas to live a pirate's life? **Turn a cardboard box into a shipshape vessel and set sail for adventure in your own room.**

MATERIALS

- 1 large rectangular cardboard box
- 1 medium size shoe box
- acrylic paint
- markers
- 2 dowels, 1/8 inch (0.3 cm) wide and 20 inches (51 cm) long
- 1 piece of black or red cloth, 8 by 10 inches (20 by 25 cm)
- 1 large paper or plastic cup

Step 1: Cut open the large box and lay it flat. Cut away the narrow section from one end. From one side, measure and cut one-third of the length along the creases on each side of the middle section as shown.

Step 2: Fold up the outer sides of the box. Bend the ends together until they touch. While holding the ends together, trace around the bottom onto the base. Lay the sides down again. Now cut along the curved lines you just made to form the bottom of the ship.

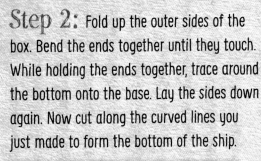

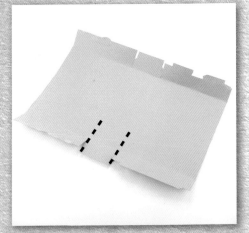

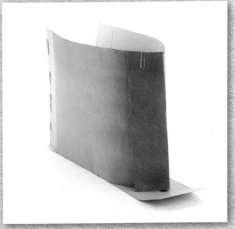

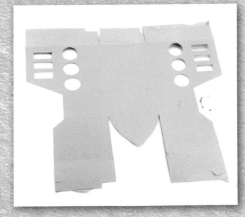

Step 3: On the flat sides, draw out the outer sides of the ship. Include railings and portholes. Cut along these marks to form the outer sides of the ship.

Step 4: Fold the sides up. Bend the front ends together and use duct tape to hold them in place. Tape along the bottom and back edges of the ship as well.

Step 5: Tape the shoe box shut. Hot glue it into the back of the ship to make the ship's deck.

Step 6: Punch a small hole into the top of the shoe box. Insert one of the dowels into the hole to make the mast. Glue it in place.

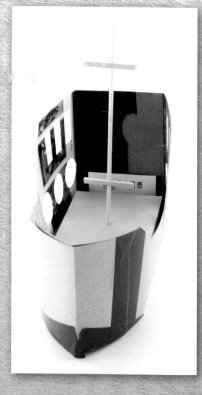

Step 7: Cut the second dowel in half. Hot glue one half about 4 inches (10 cm) from the top of the mast to make a T-shape. Glue the second half 8 inches (20 cm) below the first.

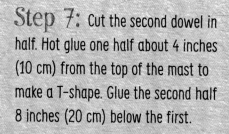

Step 8: To make a crow's nest, cut a 2-inch (5-cm) tall piece off the bottom of the plastic cup. Punch a hole through the bottom of the cup. Slide the cup piece onto the mast until it rests on the top dowel. Glue it in place.

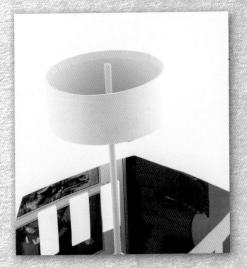

Step 9: Paint the ship, ship deck, mast, and crow's nest in any color you wish. Let everything dry completely. Use more paint or markers to decorate and add details to the ship.

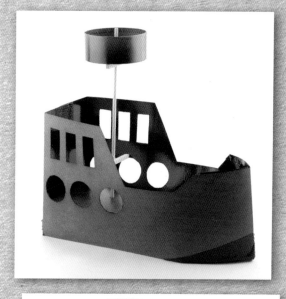

Step 10: For a pirate sail, draw a skull and crossbones on the piece of cloth in white or black marker. Glue the sail to the horizontal dowels. Shiver me timbers, you're done!

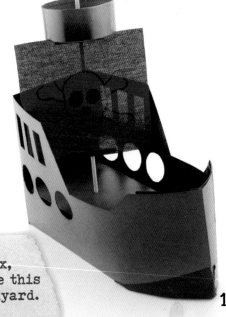

Tip: You can use a large appliance box, PVC pipes, and an old bed sheet to make this project into a huge ship for your backyard.

Incredible Life-Size Robot

Need a place to post your baseball schedule or send a message to your little brother? Just use this awesome cardboard android assistant! Have fun using dry erase markers to write messages to your family on the whiteboard body.

MATERIALS

- 1 large square cardboard box
- 1 medium square cardboard box
- 2 medium rectangular cardboard boxes
- masking tape
- silver duct tape
- 2 pieces of dryer vent hose, 20 inches (51 cm) long
- silver spray paint
- whiteboard paint
- black markers
- metal nuts, washers, bottle caps, and other objects

Step 1: Tape the cardboard boxes shut with masking tape. Place the rectangular boxes to form the robot's feet and legs. Use the large square box for the robot's chest. Use the medium square box for its head. Hot glue the boxes together. Paint the entire robot with silver spray paint and allow to dry.

Step 2: Cut holes in the sides of the chest box to fit the dryer vent hoses. Place the hoses in the holes and hot glue them in place. Tape around the joints with silver duct tape. Fold a piece of tape around the other ends of the hoses to smooth the edges.

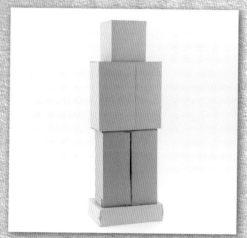

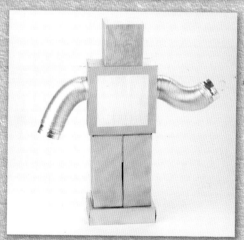

Tip: You can also paint an old pair of goggles to make cool robot eyes.

Step 3: Outline a large square on the robot's chest with masking tape. Paint this square with whiteboard paint and allow to dry. When the paint is dry, remove the tape.

Step 4: Use black markers to outline the robot's feet, legs, and message box. Attach nuts, washers, bottle caps, and other objects with hot glue to create the robot's face and controls.

17

Viking Shield and Sword

Fierce Viking warriors charged into battle with sturdy shields and swords. With just a few simple supplies, you can make your own cardboard sword and shield. Make several of these with your friends and stage your own epic adventure!

MATERIALS

- 1 large pizza pan
- 3 large flat sheets of cardboard
- black and gold paint
- 1 small aluminum or paper bowl
- silver and black duct tape
- clean milk jug with handle
- 4 buttons or bottle caps
- 1-inch (2.5-cm) wide dowel, 18 inches (46 cm) long
- fake jewels

Step 1: Trace around the pizza pan onto one large sheet of cardboard. Cut out the circle. Draw a large X on the cardboard circle to divide it into four sections. Paint the sections black and gold.

Step 2: Place strips of silver duct tape along the lines of the X. Fold duct tape around the edge of the shield.

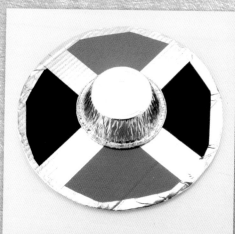

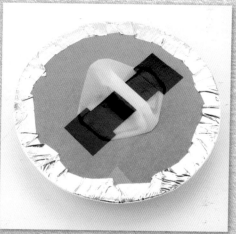

Step 3: Hot glue the small aluminum bowl upside down onto the center of the shield. Or cover a paper bowl with silver duct tape and glue it to the shield.

Step 4: Cut the handle off the milk jug. Hot glue it to the center of the back of the shield. Use duct tape to help make the handle stronger. Glue the buttons to the front of the shield in the four painted sections.

Step 5: Draw an 18-inch (46-cm) long sword shape on two sheets of cardboard. Include a 4-inch (10-cm) wide cross guard and a rounded pommel at the bottom. Cut out the sword pieces.

Step 6: Attach the dowel to the inside of one cardboard sword shape with duct tape. Then hot glue the two sword shapes together with the dowel inside.

Step 7: Cover the blade of the sword with silver duct tape. Cover the cross guard and pommel with black duct tape.

Step 8: Glue the fake jewels on the hilt of the sword for decoration.

Tip: Research Viking warriors at the library or on the Internet to get ideas for decorating your gear.

Creative Cardboard Lantern

If you like camping or cookouts after sunset, this project is for you.

A cardboard milk carton, a battery-powered candle, and some parchment paper make an awesome lantern. Take it along on your next night time hike or use it as a Halloween decoration!

MATERIALS

- cardboard milk carton
- old washcloths
- black acrylic paint
- parchment paper
- white paper
- white glue
- battery-operated tea light candle
- 2 pieces of string, 2 feet (0.6 meter) long
- decorative bead

Step 1: First paint the carton. Let it dry completely. Then ask an adult to help cut the top off the milk carton so it is 6 inches (15 cm) tall. Next, draw a line 2 inches (5 cm) below the top edge.

Step 2: Slit the corners from the top edge down to the line to make four flaps. Measure and mark the center of each flap at the top edge. Cut from the center marks down to each corner of the carton. Each flap should now be a triangle. Punch a hole in the top of each triangle.

Step 3: Stuff the washcloths into the carton to help keep it stable. Cut rectangles out of each side of the carton. Leave a 0.75-inch (2-cm) wide margin on the left and right sides. Leave a 1-inch (2.5-cm) wide margin on the top and bottom.

Step 4: Measure and cut four parchment paper rectangles to fit inside the sides of the carton. Cut designs from the white paper. Glue one design piece to the center of each parchment paper rectangle. Glue the parchment rectangles inside the carton to cover the open spaces.

Step 5: Thread the strings through the holes in the top flaps. Hold the four ends together and thread them through the decorative bead. Tie the ends of the strings into a knot.

Step 6: Slide the bead up to open the top of the lantern. Put in the battery-operated candle. Slide the bead down to close the lantern. Use the string as a hanger or a handle.

Tip: For a sports theme, make a lantern for each letter in your favorite team's name and hang them side-by-side!

Homemade Movie Projector

With this cool homemade projector, you can make your own movie theater at home!

Set up some comfortable chairs in a dark room, gather some friends, and start the show. Don't forget the popcorn!

MATERIALS

- shoe box with lid
- black paint
- small magnifying glass
- smartphone
- modeling clay

Step 1: Paint the inside of the shoe box and the lid black.

Step 2: In one end of the box, cut a hole slightly smaller than the magnifying glass.

Step 3: Use duct tape or hot glue to attach the magnifying glass over the hole inside the box.

Step 4: Put the box on a table in a dark room and point it toward an empty wall. Open a photo on the smartphone and place the phone near the opposite end of the box. Use modeling clay to hold it in place.

Step 5: Put the lid on the box. The image on the phone will be projected onto the wall. If the image is upside down, flip the phone over inside the box. Adjust the distance between the box and the wall to focus the picture. Now start a movie on the phone, kick back, and enjoy the show!

Super Solar Cooker

Summer sunshine can get pretty hot. Why not use that solar energy to make a fun lunch with your friends? With this solar cooker, you can roast hot dogs and make s'mores without even building a campfire.

MATERIALS
- clean pizza box with lid
- aluminum foil
- clear tape
- plastic wrap
- black construction paper
- newspaper

Step 1: Cover the inside bottom of the pizza box with black construction paper. The black paper helps absorb heat from the sun. Roll up sheets of newspaper and tape them around the edges inside the box. The newspaper helps insulate the cooker.

Step 2: Close the pizza box. Then measure and mark a 1-inch (2.5-cm) wide border on the front, left, and right sides of the box top. Ask an adult to help cut along the marks to make a flap. Fold the flap up.

Step 3: Cover the inside of the flap with aluminum foil. Be sure the shiny side faces out to reflect the sun.

Step 4: Tape two sheets of plastic wrap over the hole in the lid. Make sure the plastic wrap is sealed completely.

Step 5: At about noon or when the sun is hottest, open the box and place your food inside at the center. Then close the lid tightly and prop up the flap. Place the box so the flap reflects sunlight onto the food. When your food looks ready, remove and enjoy!

27

Magic Money Mover

Now you see it ... now you don't!

How does the dollar bill move from one side of the wallet to the other? With just a few simple supplies, you can create this fun magical wallet to astound your family and friends.

MATERIALS

- 1 sheet of cardboard
- 2 pieces of blue ribbon, 4 inches (10 cm) long
- 2 pieces of white ribbon, 4 inches (10 cm) long
- clear tape
- ruler
- dollar bill

Step 1: Cut two rectangles of cardboard measuring 2.75 by 4 inches (7 by 10 cm). Lay the blue ribbons across the top and bottom of one rectangle. The ribbons should be about 0.25 inch (0.6 cm) from the top and bottom edges. The ribbon ends will extend about 0.5 inch (1.3 cm) past each side.

Step 2: Place the second cardboard rectangle on top of the first so the ribbons are between them. Fold the ends of the ribbons on the right side over the top and tape in place.

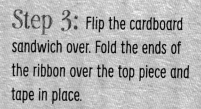

Step 3: Flip the cardboard sandwich over. Fold the ends of the ribbon over the top piece and tape in place.

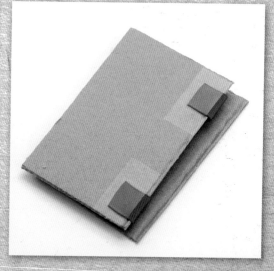

Step 4: Unfold the cardboard pieces. The ribbon will run between the rectangles. The piece on the right has ribbons taped to the underside. The piece on the left has ribbons taped to the top.

Step 5: Place the white ribbons in an X shape on the right rectangle. Tuck the ends of the white ribbon under the left rectangle.

Step 6: Flip the left rectangle over the right rectangle. Fold the ends of the white ribbon on the left side over the top and tape them down.

Step 7: Flip the whole wallet over. Fold the ends of the white ribbon on the right side over the top rectangle and tape them down.

Step 8: Open the wallet. There will be two lines of blue ribbon on the left, and an X of white ribbon on the right.

Step 9: Place a folded dollar bill on top of the X and close the wallet. Open it from left to right. The dollar moves under the X! Close the wallet and open it from left to right again. The dollar bill moves to the other side.

Tip: Cover the backsides of the magic wallet with colored paper to hide the taped ribbon ends.

Colossal Cardboard Ball

Here's a riddle for you. What do you get when you join 30 flat cardboard squares at the corners? A big sphere! This cardboard ball is not only super cool, it's quick and easy to make.

MATERIALS

- 30 squares of sturdy cardboard, 10 by 10 inches (25 by 25 cm)
- 60 brass fasteners

Step 1: Punch a hole in each corner of all the cardboard squares.

Step 2: Use brass fasteners to join five squares at the corners to make a pentagon-shaped space in the center.

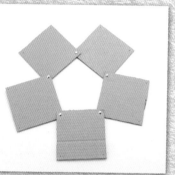

Step 3: On the outer corners of the first squares, add more squares to make triangle-shaped spaces between them.

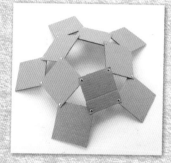

Step 4: Continue adding squares until you have used all 30. Arrange them so the spaces alternate between pentagons and triangles. Gently curve each row of squares until you have a sphere shape.

Tip: Take your colossal ball outside on a windy day and watch as the air pushes it along. It seems to almost move by itself!

Secret Book Box

Do you have any treasures you want to keep hidden? **Stash them safely in this nifty secret book box. Nobody will find your stuff in this super-secret hiding spot!**

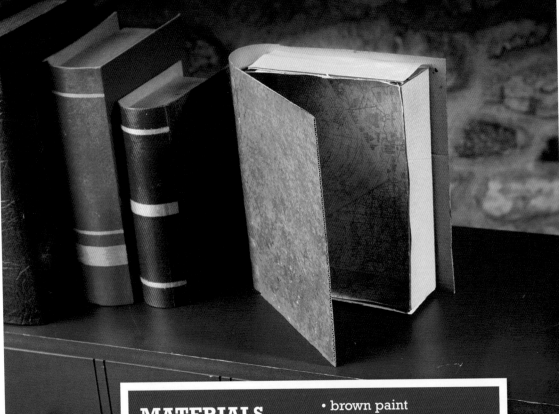

MATERIALS

- 1 book-sized box, such as a cracker box or small cereal box
- clear tape
- 1 cardboard paper towel tube
- 1 large sheet of sturdy cardboard
- brown paint
- sponge
- silver or gold paint
- paintbrush
- colored paper
- white paper
- black pen
- glue or spray adhesive

Step 1: Close the top of the box and tape it shut. Cut along three sides of the front of the box so it opens like a book.

Step 2: Cut the cardboard tube along its length. Measure the side of the box. Cut the cardboard tube to be 0.5 inch (1.3 cm) longer and 1 inch (2.5 cm) wider than the side of the box. Measure the front of the box. Cut two rectangles from the cardboard sheet to be 0.25 inch (0.6 cm) longer and wider than the box. These pieces will be used for the front, back, and spine of the book.

Step 3: Use a sponge and brown paint to cover the cardboard pieces so they look like leather. Paint gold or silver stripes on the spine.

Step 4: Measure and cut pieces of colored paper to fit the inside surfaces of the box. Use spray adhesive or glue to attach the colored paper inside the box.

35

Step 5: Measure and cut strips of white paper to fit the top, bottom, and outside edges of the box. Draw thin lines on the paper with a black pen to look like pages of a book. Glue the paper strips to the outside edges of the box.

Step 6: Glue one cover piece to the front flap of the box. Be sure to line up the back edge of the cover with the back edge of the box. The cover will extend a bit beyond the other edges of the box. Repeat this step with the second cover piece on the back of the box.

Step 7: Use clear tape to attach the spine piece to the back of the box. Now put your secret stuff inside the box and hide it on a bookshelf!

Tip: To make your secret book even more realistic, print out a cover and paste it to the front of the box.

Giant Cardboard Fortress

Lords and ladies of the kingdom need a cool place to hang out. Collect large cardboard boxes and tubes to make your own fortress. Use appliance boxes to make your fortress big enough for some knights and their horses too.

MATERIALS

- 4 large cardboard refrigerator boxes
- several large flat sheets of cardboard
- large cardboard tubes
- tissue boxes
- duct tape
- heavy string
- light gray paint
- red or blue paint
- thick black markers

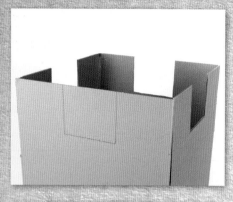

Step 1: Use the refrigerator boxes to make the corner towers of the fortress. Open the tops and use duct tape to hold the side flaps open. Measure and mark a line 5 inches (13 cm) from the top on each side. Measure and mark 6-inch (15-cm) long rectangles along the line. Cut out every other rectangle to make fortress battlements.

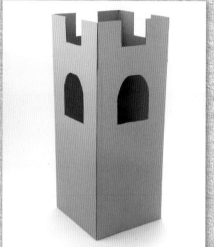

Step 2: Draw arched windows on the outer walls of the towers. Cut them out. Use duct tape to attach the flat sheets of cardboard between the towers to form fortress walls.

Step 3: Draw and cut out a large arched door on the front of the fortress. Leave the base of the door uncut to make a drawbridge.

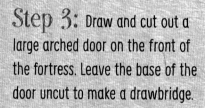

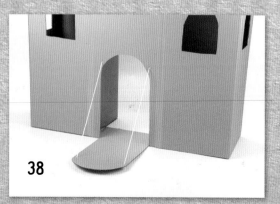

Step 4: Punch holes on each side of the doorway and at the top of the drawbridge as shown. Tie strings to the top of the drawbridge and thread them through the holes above the doorway. Tie knots in the ends of the strings to hold them in place.

Step 5: Add flagpoles to the fortress by taping the cardboard tubes to the top of the walls. To make flags, cut out cardboard flag shapes and glue or tape them to the cardboard tubes.

Step 6: Add balconies to some windows by taping tissue boxes beneath them.

Step 7: Paint the entire castle light gray. Paint the flags red or blue.

Step 8: When the paint is dry, draw rectangle shapes with a thick black marker to look like stone blocks. You can also add royal emblems and crests to the flags. Now gather your friends together to help defend the fortress and your kingdom!

Armored Knight Costume

Thinking of joining in on some cardboard combat? This cardboard armor can help protect you. Suit up and get ready for battle!

MATERIALS

- cardboard box about the size of your upper body
- large paper plate
- pencil
- silver duct tape
- silver paint
- black marker
- string
- buttons or bottle caps

Step 1: Cut off one short side of the cardboard box. Using the plate as a pattern, draw a circle on the other short side large enough for your head. Cut out the circle.

Step 2: Put the cardboard on over your head like a poncho. Have a friend draw lines to mark out the waistline and armholes. Take the box off and cut the cardboard at the markings. The box should now look like an undershirt.

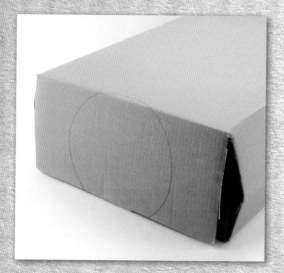

Step 3: Try on the armor shirt and bend the sides to adjust it as needed. Use duct tape to hold the sides together if necessary.

Step 4: Paint the armor silver. Use markers to add a crest or logo to the front.

Step 5: For the helmet, use a piece of string to measure around your head. Cut four 1-inch (2.5-cm) wide strips of cardboard to the measured length. Hot glue the ends of one strip together to make a hoop that fits around your head. There should be a little wiggle room.

Step 6: Bend another cardboard strip into an upside down U shape. Glue the ends to the inside of the circle to form the top of the helmet. Repeat with another cardboard strip. Make it cross the first strip at the center top of the helmet. Trim away the ends that hang down under the edge of the circle.

Step 7: Cut a 3-inch (7.6-cm) wide cardboard circle. Glue it under the cross point at the top of the helmet.

Step 8: Cut four triangles with rounded corners to fit inside the open spaces in the frame. Hot glue them to the inside of the frame.

Step 9: Cut a U-shaped piece of cardboard to use as a face shield. Cut smaller U shapes for eyeholes.

Step 10: Hot glue the face shield inside the front of the helmet rim. Glue a strip of 1-inch (2.5-cm) wide cardboard between the eyeholes to form a nose guard.

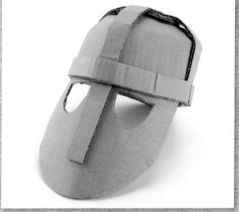

Step 11: Hot glue metal buttons or bottle caps to look like rivets in the helmet frame. Paint the helmet silver and let it dry. Now put on your armor and helmet, grab your sword and shield, and get ready for battle!

Tip: To make the armor more flexible, try cutting open the box sides. Then punch holes in the sides and lace them together with heavy string.

Create
Incredible
Duct Tape Projects!

It's strong, flexible, waterproof, and super sticky. People use it to fix everything from windows and boats to baseball bats. Some people even use it to make warts disappear. What is this awesome stuff? It's duct tape!

First made from sticky cotton fabric, soldiers once used this tape to seal boxes of ammunition. Duct tape later got its name when builders used it to hold the joints of air ducts together.

This amazing tape is great for fixing things, but it's also a popular craft supply. It comes in many colors and patterns and can be used to make all sorts of cool projects. Grab a few rolls of duct tape and get ready to make awesome laser swords, superhero helmets, and many other incredible projects!

Making Duct Tape Fabric

Some projects are made with duct tape fabric. To make this, first lay a strip of duct tape face up on your work surface. Then add a second strip by overlapping the long edge 0.25 inch (0.6 cm). Repeat this with more strips of tape until the fabric is wide enough. Then place strips of tape sticky-side-down to cover the first layer.

Awesome Laser Sword

Heading out to battle evil aliens? Smart space warriors never leave home without their trusty laser sword. With some colorful duct tape and cardboard tubes, you can make one of your own! Fight intergalactic battles with friends, or you can add a hooded cape for a cool Halloween costume.

MATERIALS

- 40-inch (102-cm) long cardboard giftwrap tube
- 9-inch (23-cm) long cardboard paper towel tube
- two 12- by 12-inch (30- by 30-cm) squares of aluminum foil
- glow-in-the-dark duct tape
- silver duct tape
- black duct tape
- red duct tape

Step 1: First crumple one square of aluminum foil into a ball about as wide as the long tube. Use hot glue to secure the foil ball halfway inside the end of the tube.

Step 2: Next cover the rounded end of the tube with two 4-inch (10-cm) long strips of glow-in-the-dark duct tape. Then cover the rest of the tube with long strips of glow-in-the-dark tape.

Step 3: Crumple the second square of foil into a ball. Hot glue it to one end of the short tube. Cover the round end with two 4-inch (10-cm) long strips of silver duct tape. Then cover the length of this tube with silver duct tape.

Step 4: Cut two or three 5-inch (13-cm) long strips of black duct tape in various widths. Use these to add stripes to the short tube.

Step 5: Tape four small squares of red duct tape onto the tube to make buttons, switches, and controls.

Step 6: Slide the short tube onto the open end of the long tube. If it doesn't fit snugly, use hot glue to keep it in place. Now you're ready to save the galaxy!

Tip: Try giving your laser sword 3-D buttons, switches, and controls. Use hot glue to attach craft foam cutouts to the handle. Then cover them with squares of colored duct tape.

Super Tri-Fold Wallet

Would you like a colorful, waterproof wallet that shows your personality? This cool wallet can be made from your favorite colors. Or you can even create your own superhero logo. Use it to safely stash your cash before taking off to save the world.

MATERIALS

- silver duct tape
- green duct tape
- white duct tape
- black duct tape
- clear plastic freezer bag

Step 1: Make two pieces of 4- by 10-inch (10- by 25-cm) silver duct tape fabric.

....

Step 2: Lay the two pieces on top of each other. Fold a 10-inch (25-cm) long strip of duct tape over the bottom to join the two pieces together. Then fold a 4-inch (10-cm) long strip of duct tape over each side to join the two sides. Leave the wallet open on top.

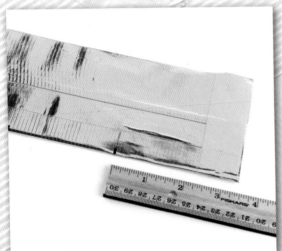

Step 3: Lay a ruler along the bottom of the wallet. With a pen or pencil, make a mark a little less than 3.5 inches (9 cm) from the left side. Make another mark about 3.5 inches (9 cm) from the right side. Fold the right side of the wallet in to make a crease. Do the same on the left side. Place a heavy book on the wallet to squeeze the creases tighter. Leave the book on the wallet for at least one hour.

Step 4: Make two more pieces of duct tape fabric measuring 2 by 3.75 inches (5 by 9.5 cm). Measure and mark 1 inch (2.5 cm) from the right edge of the wallet. Attach the right side of one fabric piece at the mark with a 0.5-inch (1.3-cm) wide strip of tape.

Step 5: Place the second fabric piece on top of the first. Line up the right side with the right edge of the wallet. Use 0.5-inch (1.3-cm) wide strips of tape to attach the fabric pieces at the top, bottom, and right edges. Leave the left sides open to form pockets for the wallet.

Step 6: Repeat steps 4 and 5 on the left third of the wallet.

Step 7: Cut a rectangle measuring 2.5 by 3.75 inches (6 by 9.5 cm) from the plastic bag. Fold a 0.5-inch (1.3-cm) wide strip of tape over one long edge of the plastic. Use more strips of tape to attach the plastic to the center of the wallet. Leave the top edge open to create a clear pocket.

Step 8: Cut your first initial or a superhero logo from green duct tape. Stick the logo onto white duct tape and cut around the shape to create a border. Stick this piece onto a black circle. Stick the circle to the front to finish your wallet.

Tip: You could also try using your favorite sports team's colors and logo for your wallet.

Cool, Colorful Kite

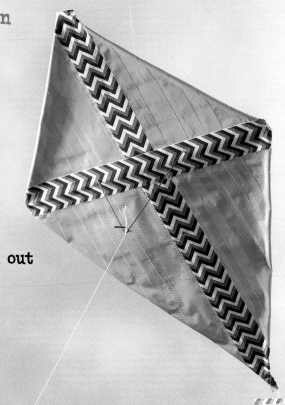

What do Benjamin Franklin and Charlie Brown have in common? They both flew kites! Become a member of the kite flyers club by making your own duct tape kite. Use bright colors to make your kite stand out against the blue sky.

MATERIALS

- 1/8-inch (0.3-cm) wide dowel, 36 inches (91 cm) long
- 1/8-inch (0.3-cm) wide dowel, 33 inches (84 cm) long
- black marker
- large spool of strong string
- colorful duct tape
- large plastic garbage bag

Step 1: Measure 10 inches (25 cm) from the top of the longer dowel and make a mark. Measure and mark the exact center of the shorter dowel.

Step 2: Place the dowels together where they are marked to form a "T" shape. Cut a 12-inch (30.5-cm) long piece of the string. Start 3 inches (8 cm) from the end of the string and wind it around the point where the dowels cross. Tightly wind the string around both dowels in a repeating "X" pattern. Tightly tie the two ends of the string together. To make the connection extra sturdy, wrap a small piece of duct tape around the string.

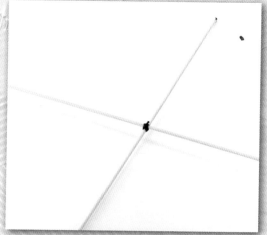

Step 3: Cut two sides of the garbage bag so it is a single sheet of plastic. Lay the kite frame on the sheet of plastic. Draw a kite shape around it with the marker. Leave a 1-inch (2.5-cm) wide margin beyond the ends of the dowels.

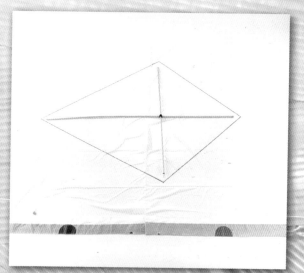

Step 4: Turn over the plastic sheet. Cover the plastic where the kite shape is drawn with strips of duct tape. Be sure to overlap the strips by 0.25 inch (0.6 cm).

Step 5: Flip the plastic over again. Cut out the kite shape. Lay the kite frame on the kite and tape the dowels in place. Fold in the margin around the edges of the kite and over the ends of the dowels. Tape the edges down with small strips of duct tape. Make the corners neat by folding them in before folding in the sides.

Step 6: On the horizontal dowel, make marks 6 inches (15 cm) from the vertical dowel on each side. Punch small holes through the kite at both marks.

Step 7: Tie the end of a 28-inch (71-cm) long piece of string to the horizontal dowel at one mark. Thread the string through the holes in the kite. Tie the other end of the string to the horizontal dowel at the second mark.

Step 8: Cut an 18-inch (46-cm) long piece of duct tape in half lengthwise. Stick the end of one piece onto the second to make a 36-inch (91-cm) long piece. Fold the tape in half lengthwise to make a tail.

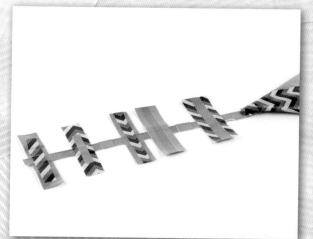

Step 9: Cut six 6-inch (15-cm) long pieces of duct tape in half lengthwise. Place them on the tail 5 inches (13 cm) apart with the tail sandwiched between them. Then tape the tail to the bottom of the kite.

Step 10: Tie the spool of flying string to the center of the front string on the kite. Now find a wide open, windy space to fly your new kite!

Easy Travel Checkers Set

Need something fun to do on a long car trip? Turn a clean pizza box into a cool checkers set before you hit the road. The checkerboard doubles as a lid, and you can store the playing pieces inside the box. You could even throw some playing cards and a good book in there too!

MATERIALS

- clean 10- by 10-inch (25- by 25-cm) pizza box
- black duct tape
- red duct tape
- 24 water bottle caps

Step 1: Cut a 14-inch (36-cm) long strip of red duct tape. Fold it in half lengthwise with the sticky sides together. Repeat this step to make eight red strips and eight black strips.

Step 2: Lay the eight strips of red tape side-by-side on a flat surface. Use a strip of tape to hold them down on one end. Now weave the black strips through the red strips to form a checkerboard.

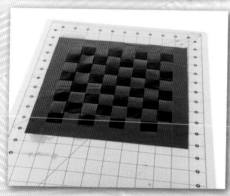

Step 3: Place red tape on the sides of the checkerboard to hold everything in place. Trim each side so it's 1 inch (2.5 cm) wider than the checkerboard.

Step 4: Use red tape to attach the checkerboard to the top of the pizza box. Use black tape to cover the sides of the pizza box.

Step 5: Next cut 1- by 1-inch (2.5- by 2.5-cm) squares of duct tape. Make 12 red squares and 12 black squares. Stick the squares to the tops of the bottle caps and smooth the corners down. Cut 0.25- by 4-inch (0.6- by 10-cm) strips of red and black duct tape. Use these to cover the sides of the caps. Trim off any excess tape. Store the checkers inside the box.

Sports Trivia Game

Are you a sports trivia whiz? Round up a couple of friends and show off your knowledge with this cool duct tape sports trivia game.

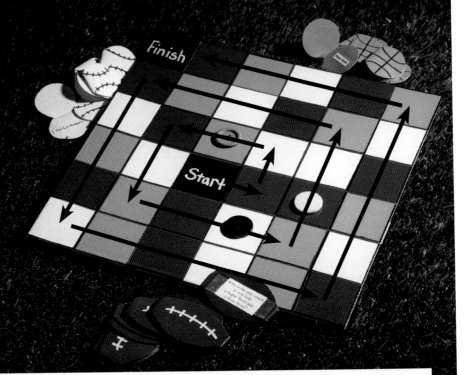

MATERIALS

- brown duct tape
- white duct tape
- orange duct tape
- black duct tape
- white permanent marker
- red permanent marker
- black permanent marker
- clear tape
- 24- by 24-inch (61- by 61-cm) sheet of cardboard
- dice
- different colored buttons

Step 1: Make 10 football game cards by sticking two 2- by 6-inch (5- by 15-cm) strips of brown duct tape together. Fold this piece in half so it's 2 by 3 inches (5 by 7.5 cm). Cut it into the shape of a football. Leave the center of the folded side uncut. Mark stitches on one side with the white marker.

Step 2: Make 10 baseball game cards by sticking two 2- by 4-inch (5- by 10-cm) strips of white duct tape together. Fold this piece in half so it's 2 by 2 inches (5 by 5 cm). Cut it into a circle. Leave the center of the folded side uncut. Mark stitches on one side with the red marker.

Step 3: Using orange duct tape, repeat step 2 to make 10 basketball game cards. Mark stitches with the black marker.

Step 4: Use a computer and printer to print sports trivia questions and answers. For example, use records such as "Most Home Runs in a Season" or "Most Rushing Touchdowns in a Single Game." Cut the questions out and attach them to the back side of the cards with clear tape. Attach the answers to the inside of the cards.

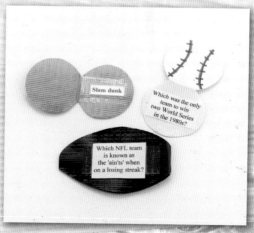

Slam dunk

Which was the only team to win two World Series in the 1980s?

Which NFL team is known as the 'ain'ts' when on a losing streak?

Step 5: To make the game board, mark a grid of 2- by 2-inch (5- by 5-cm) squares on the cardboard. Place 2- by 2-inch (5- by 5-cm) squares of black tape at the center and top left corner squares of the board. Alternately place brown, white, and orange squares of tape to make a square spiral shape around the board. Mark the START and FINISH squares with white marker. Draw arrows with black marker to show what direction to move the buttons.

Step 6: To play the game, stack the game cards by the game board so you can't see the questions. Place the buttons on the START square. Players take turns rolling a die and moving their buttons. Players pick cards matching the color of the spaces they land on. If players answer questions correctly, they may take another turn. If players answer incorrectly, they must return to the square where they started their turn. The next player then takes his or her turn. The player who makes it to the FINISH square first is the winner!

Tip: Find sports trivia questions on the Internet or at your local library.

Pirate Booty Treasure Chest

Aarrr! Shiver me timbers! Every pirate needs a safe place to store secret loot. Keep land lovers from snooping into your stuff with this duct tape treasure chest. Add a skull and crossbones or "KEEP OUT" sign so curious siblings know you mean business.

MATERIALS

- plain cardboard box with hinged lid
- wood grain duct tape
- black duct tape
- brass fasteners
- large washer
- small padlock

Step 1: Cover the box and lid with wood grain duct tape.

Step 2: Use black duct tape to cover the edges of the box. Make a black stripe down the center of the box as well.

Step 3: Measure and make several evenly spaced marks along the black stripes. Punch small holes into the box at each mark.

Step 4: Push a brass fastener into each hole. On the inside of the box, bend the ends of the fasteners out flat.

Tip: If you can't find a box with a hinged lid, you can use a regular shoe box with a lid. Cut away the overhang on one long side of the lid. Then attach it to the box with black duct tape.

Step 5: Make a 1-inch (2.5-cm) long mark at the front center of the box, just under the lid. Cut a slit at this mark to insert the washer.

....

Step 6: Cover the washer with black duct tape. Leave the hole open in the middle. Use hot glue to attach the washer in place inside the box.

....

Step 7: Make a 2- by 3-inch (5- by 7.5-cm) piece of black duct tape fabric. Cut a slit in the piece to fit over the washer on the front of the box. Attach this piece inside the front center of the lid. Now just add your secret loot and lock it up to keep it safe!

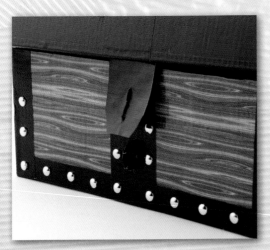

Hot Beats Bongo Drums

Every band needs a drummer! Use this set of bongo drums to play some great music with your friends. Tap the drums with your fingertips and the palms of your hands. Or for a different sound, try using drumsticks or chopsticks.

MATERIALS

- 1 medium oatmeal container
- 1 large oatmeal container
- white, tan, and black duct tape
- brass fasteners
- small block of wood,
    2 by 1.5 by 1.5 inches
    (5 by 3.8 by 3.8 cm)

Step 1: Remove the lids and turn the containers upside down. Cover the bottoms of the containers with white duct tape. Cut strips long enough to cross the center and overlap the sides of the containers about 1 inch (2.5 cm). Cover the sides of the drums with vertical stripes of tan and black duct tape.

Step 2: Cut a strip of white tape long enough to fit around the drum with a 2-inch (5-cm) overlap. Fold it in half lengthwise with the sticky sides together. Make two strips for each drum.

Step 3: Measure and mark about 1.5 inches (3.8 cm) from the top and bottom edges of each drum. Attach the white strips at the marks with a bit of tape. Punch small holes through the white strip and the drum at the center of each tan stripe. Push brass fasteners through the holes. Flatten the fasteners inside the drums.

Step 4: Cover the block of wood with a piece of black duct tape. Hot glue the two drums on each side of the wood block. Now you're ready to lay down some awesome beats!

Tip: Coffee cans and cornmeal containers make good drums too. For the best sound, leave the bottom of the drum open.

Cool Camo Belt

Why wear a plain black belt when you can take it up a notch? Make your own fashion statement by wearing this cool homemade camouflage belt.

MATERIALS

- camouflage duct tape
- metal belt buckle with prong
- string

Step 1: Stick two 4-inch (10-cm) long strips of duct tape together with the sticky side in. Measure the width of the inside of the buckle. Trim the strip of tape to the same width. Punch a small hole for the prong of the buckle.

Step 2: Slide the tape through the buckle and insert the prong into the hole.

Step 3: Measure a piece of string to fit around your waist. Add an extra 4 inches (10 cm) to the end. Use the string to measure two long strips of duct tape.

Step 4: Attach the buckle piece to the end of one long strip. Place the second long strip on top of the first with the sticky sides facing in. Trim the long tape to match the width of the buckle piece.

Step 5: Fold a 4-inch (10 cm) long strip of tape in half lengthwise. Wrap it around the belt 0.5 inch (1.3 cm) from the buckle. Tape this piece in place on the back side of the belt to form a loop.

Step 6: Punch several holes at the end of the belt. Space them 1 inch (2.5 cm) apart. Try on your belt and trim away the end if it's too long.

Tip: Look for old belts at thrift shops to find cool buckles you can reuse.

Sports Team Ball Cap

Heading to the ballpark? Don't forget your duct tape cap! Choose duct tape that matches your team's colors. Then add a logo to make your cap stand out in the crowd.

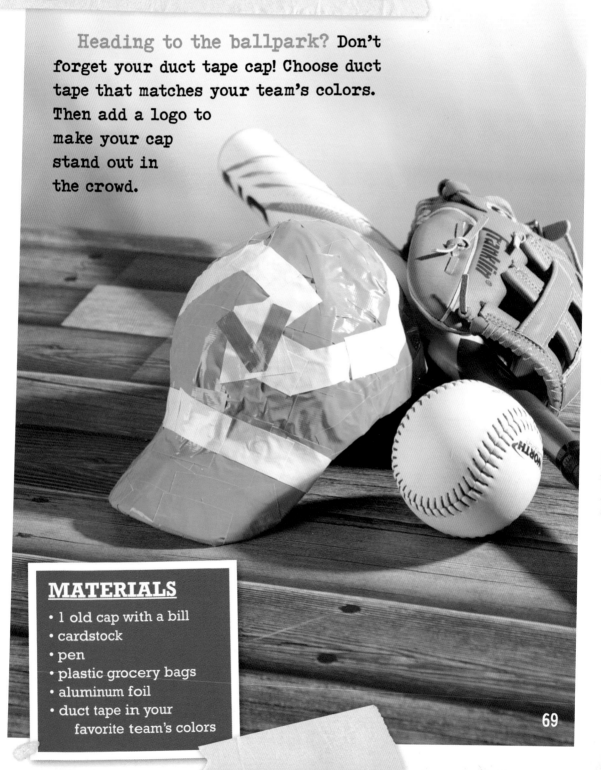

MATERIALS

- 1 old cap with a bill
- cardstock
- pen
- plastic grocery bags
- aluminum foil
- duct tape in your favorite team's colors

Step 1: Trace the bill of the cap onto a piece of cardstock. Cut out the cardboard bill.

Step 2: Adjust the cap to fit your head. Then stuff the inside of the cap with crumpled plastic bags to hold it's shape. Mold a large sheet of aluminum foil over the top of the cap. Fold the edges to the inside.

Step 3: Cover the foil with 2-inch (5-cm) squares of duct tape. Overlap and smooth the squares to completely cover the foil. The edges of the duct tape should go a little beyond the edges of the hat.

Step 4: Turn the hat upside down and remove the plastic bags. Unfold the foil from the edges of the hat and gently pull the hat away from the foil.

Step 5: Use a few bits of tape to attach the cardstock bill to the inside of the foil.

Step 6: Cover the bill and the inside of the hat with 2-inch (5-cm) squares of overlapping duct tape.

Step 7: Cut out a duct tape team logo and add it to the front of the cap. Now you're ready to cheer on your favorite team in style!

Tip: To make a slightly smaller cap, begin by molding the foil to the inside of the cap instead of the outside.

Incredible Superhero Helmet

Want to be a superhero? What would your super power be? Flying? Super speed? Leaping over skyscrapers? Whatever it is, you can show it off with your own personal duct tape superhero helmet!

MATERIALS

- duct tape in your favorite colors
- plastic grocery bag
- sturdy foam head stand

Step 1: Cut several 5-inch (13-cm) long strips of duct tape and several 2-inch (5-cm) squares of duct tape. Place the tape on a cutting board so they're ready to use.

....

Step 2: Fit the grocery bag over the foam head stand. Cut away the plastic so it covers the hair and forehead areas, but not the face. (Safety note: Plastic bags can be dangerous. Never place a plastic bag over your own head or anyone else's head.)

Step 3: Cover the plastic bag with the strips of duct tape.

Step 4: Cut a mask out of the leftover plastic to go over the eyes and top of the nose. Cut out eyeholes in the mask.

Step 5: Tape the mask to the front of the helmet at the sides.

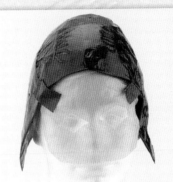

Step 6: Cover the plastic mask with small strips of duct tape in a different color. Trim the edges of the helmet into whatever shape you want.

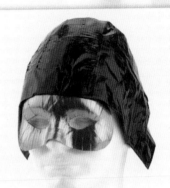

Step 7: It's time to personalize! You can add duct tape initials, logos, or numbers to the sides of the helmet. Use your imagination to create the coolest helmet you can think of. When you're done, put on your helmet and head out to save the world!

74

Tip: Cut out cardboard shapes and cover them with duct tape to make horns or antennae. Then tape them to the top of the helmet.

#1 Sports Fan Glove

Do you love those giant hands that people wave around at sporting events? You can make your own in your favorite team's colors from bubble wrap and duct tape. Take this to the next game to show your team spirit.

MATERIALS

- 2 sheets of cardstock 8.5 by 11 inches (22 by 28 cm)
- clear tape
- pen or marker
- 4 sheets of bubble wrap, about 10 by 18 inches (25 by 46 cm)
- double-sided tape
- duct tape in your favorite team's colors

Step 1: Tape the long sides of two sheets of cardstock together with clear tape.

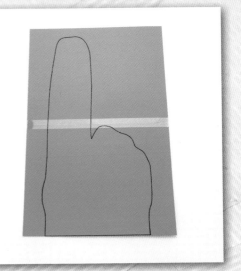

Step 2: Draw a large hand on the cardstock. Make it with the number 1 finger pointing up. Cut out the hand to use for a pattern.

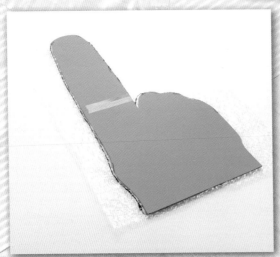

Step 3: Trace the pattern onto the four sheets of bubble wrap. Cut the hands out.

Step 4: Tape two of the bubble wrap hands together with double-sided tape. Repeat for the other two hands. Then lay the two sets of hands on top of one another.

Step 5: Cut several strips of duct tape 2 to 3 inches (5 to 7.6 cm) longer than the width of the hands.

Step 6: Fold a strip of duct tape over the bottom edge of the top layer of hands. Place it so that half of the strip goes inside the glove. Repeat this step with the bottom layer of hands.

Step 7: Cover the outside of the glove with duct tape. Fold the strips of tape around the edges to hold the layers of bubble wrap together. Overlap the edges of the duct tape for a smooth finish.

Step 8: Add a large "#1" to the front of the glove in a different color of duct tape. Now go cheer your team on to victory!

Tip: You can find sheets of bubble wrap in shipping supply sections of department stores.

Make Amazing Paper Projects!

Take a look around you and see all the ways paper is used. What would the world be like without it? There would be no lunch bags, no tissues, no newspapers, and no printed books!

But paper wasn't always an easy material to find. It was first invented in China around 200 BC. And it wasn't commonly used until the invention of the printing press in 1456. But soon the paper industry took off, and paper mills were built across Europe and the United States.

Today paper is found almost everywhere and is often used to make many fun crafts. You don't always need to buy special paper to build great projects. Look around to see what kind of paper you have at home to make paper puzzles, lanterns, models, and even an awesome space station! Let's get started!

Floating Paper Boat

Paper normally isn't very sturdy in water. But with this project you can make a paper boat that actually floats! Build a fleet of these paper boats and get ready to set sail.

MATERIALS
- 8.5- by 11-inch (22- by 28-cm) waterproof paper
- toothpicks
- glue

Step 1: Fold the paper in half. Then fold the paper in half in the opposite direction and unfold.

Step 2: Fold the top corners in to the center.

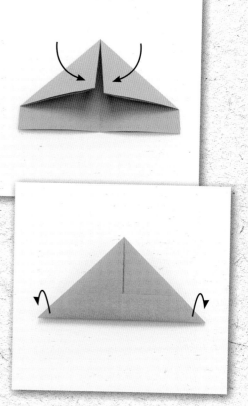

Step 3: Fold the front bottom flap over the base of the triangle. Repeat behind.

Step 4: Fold the corners of the front flap over and tuck them behind the triangle. Turn the model over. Fold the corners of flap over the back.

Step 5: Hold the triangle at the center fold. Pull the sides out to make a diamond shape.

Step 6: Fold the front bottom half of the diamond up. Repeat behind to form a new triangle.

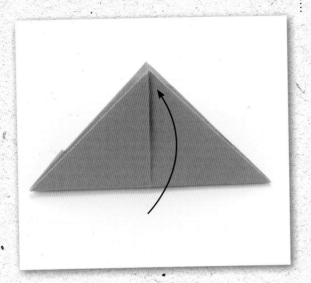

Step 7: Hold the triangle at the center and pull the sides apart to make a second diamond shape.

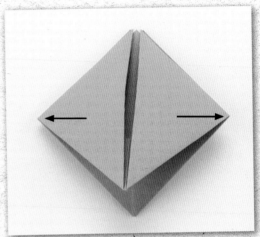

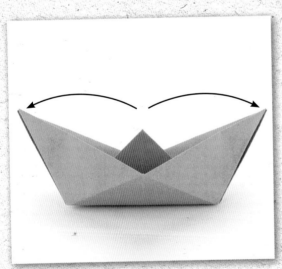

Step 8: To unfold the boat, pull apart the top points of the outer layer of the diamond. Use your finger to form the triangle in the center into a cone shape.

Step 9: Cut out and glue a small triangle of paper to a toothpick. Glue the toothpick to the boat's center cone to make a sail.

Tricky Finger Trap

Fool your friends and family with this fun gadget. It's simple to make and fun to use. A few strips of colored paper are all you need. Your friends won't know why it's easy to get their fingers in, but hard to get them out!

MATERIALS

- 4 strips of paper, 1.25 by 11 inches (3 by 28 cm) in two colors
- 1 marker, the size of a person's finger
- clear tape
- rubber band (optional)

Step 1: Fold a 0.5-inch (1.3-cm) wide flap lengthwise on a strip of paper.

Step 2: Fold a second 0.25-inch (0.6-cm) wide flap over the top of the first flap. Repeat steps 1 and 2 with the other strips of paper.

Step 3: Take a strip of each color and place the ends together at a right angle. Tuck one strip under the top flap of the other. Tape the ends together. Repeat for the second set of strips.

Step 4: Attach the taped end of one set of strips to the top front of the marker. Repeat with the second set of strips on the back side of the marker. If necessary, use a rubber band to help hold the paper strips in place.

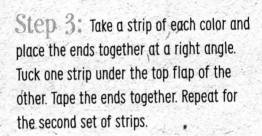

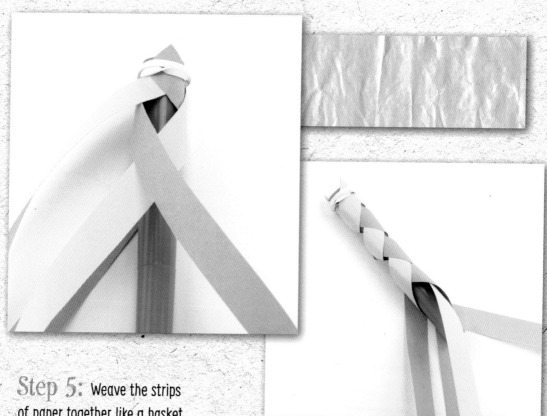

Step 5: Weave the strips of paper together like a basket. Continue weaving around and down the length of the marker.

Step 6: When finished weaving, remove the marker. Tape the ends of the strips together so they don't come apart. Now have a friend try out the finger trap and see if they can escape from it!

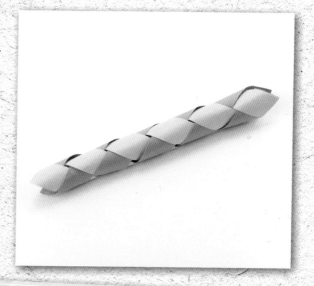

Tip: The secret to the trap is to not pull on the ends. When you pull on the ends, the strips of paper become tighter. To escape the trap, push in the ends to loosen it.

Giant Wind Spinners

Planning a fun-filled get-together or party? With some colorful paper, small dowels, and pins, you can create a festive party mood. Line your yard or porch with these giant spinners and watch the wind make them twirl.

MATERIALS

- colorful craft paper, 12 by 12 inches (30.5 by 30.5 cm)
- wooden dowels
- rectangular erasers
- pins with round heads
- buttons
- glue

Step 1: Glue two sheets of paper back to back and allow to dry. Draw a large X on the paper, with the lines crossing at the center. Cut diagonal lines from each corner about halfway to the center of the square.

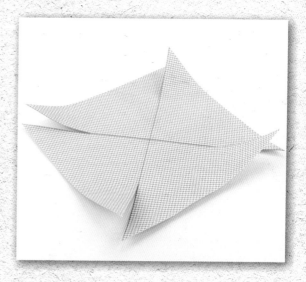

Step 2: Punch a small hole in the upper left corner, just under the cut. Turn the paper and repeat for each corner. Punch a fifth hole in the center of the paper.

Step 3: Cut a 0.5- by 1-inch (1.3- by 2.5-cm) piece off the eraser. Carefully carve a small hole with a craft knife in one side to fit the dowel. Place the eraser on the dowel.

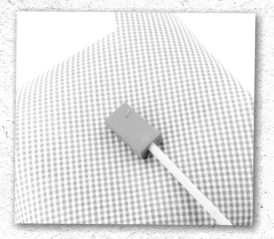

Step 4: Bend the four corners of the paper to the center and line up all the holes. Place the button over the corners. Push the pin through the button and the holes.

Step 5: Stick the pin through the eraser and out the other side. Use pliers to bend the point of the pin back against the eraser.

Happy Chinese Lanterns

In China people welcome the New Year by hanging lanterns to light the way to a happy future. You can make these lanterns using any colorful paper you have around the house. Add battery tea lights and light up your room or yard when the Sun sets.

MATERIALS
- heavy colorful paper, 8.5 by 11 inches (22 by 28 cm)
- clear tape
- clear plastic cups
- battery-operated tea light candles

Step 1: For each lantern, cut a 1-inch (2.5-cm) wide strip from the short end of the paper. Save the strips for the lantern handles.

Step 2: Fold the sheet of paper in half lengthwise. From the folded edge, measure and mark several lines 3.25 inches (8.3 cm) long. Make the lines about 1 inch (2.5 cm) apart. Cut along the lines. Be sure to stop cutting at the ends of the lines.

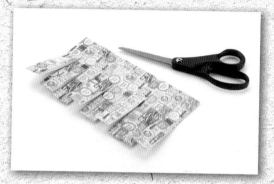

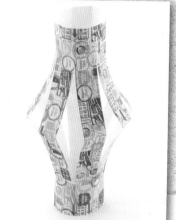

Step 3: Unfold the sheet of paper and roll it into a tube. Overlap the uncut ends and tape them together. Push together the top and bottom of the tube to spread out the lantern sections.

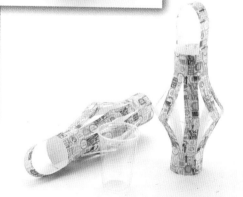

Step 4: Place a plastic cup into the bottom of the tube. Tape it in place. Tape or glue the strip of paper from step 1 to the top of the lantern to form a handle.

Step 5: Turn on a battery-powered tea light and place it inside the plastic cup.

Tip: Make several lanterns and hang them from a long string or wire outside after dark.

Awesome Space Station

What is that huge gray globe hanging from your ceiling? Is it a space station? Or is it a giant space-based super weapon? Either way, it's an awesome spacecraft—made by you!

MATERIALS

- 1 sheet of paper, 8.5 by 11 inches (22 by 28 cm)
- 1 8-inch (20-cm) wide paper plate
- 20 sheets of heavy paper or cardstock (silver or gray)
- piece of string, 4 feet (1.2 meters) long
- paper clip
- glue

Step 1: Place the paper plate on a piece of paper and draw a circle around it. Cut out the circle.

Step 2: Fold the circle in half. Then fold it into thirds and crease the folds. It should look like a slice of pie. Unfold the circle.

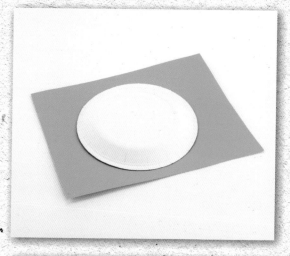

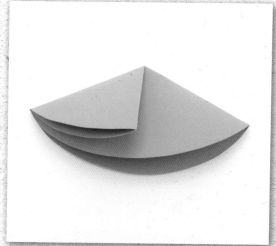

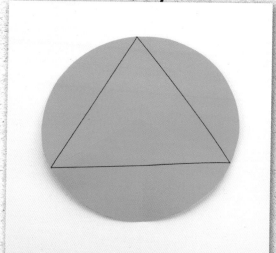

Step 3: Mark every other end point of the fold lines on the circle. Use a ruler to draw straight lines between the points to make an equilateral triangle. Cut out the triangle. This will be your pattern.

Step 4: Use the paper plate to draw circles on the 20 sheets of silver paper. Cut out the circles. Use the triangle pattern to lightly draw triangles inside the circles. Fold each circle along the triangle lines.

Step 5: For the top of the station, glue five circles together along the folded edges. This will make a circular shape. Repeat with five more circles to make the station bottom.

Step 6: Glue the remaining ten circles side by side to form a straight line.

Step 7: Glue the two ends together to form a ring. Then glue the top and bottom pieces to the ring to form a sphere. Do not glue the last two sides together yet.

Step 8: Tie the string to a paper clip. Glue the paper clip in place inside the station. Leave the rest of the string outside the sphere. Glue the final two sides together and allow all the glue to dry completely. Now just hang your space station in your room for an awesome decoration.

Tip: You can make your space station more realistic by using markers to add details like seams, bolts, doors, and hangar bays.

Puzzling Paper Cubes

How do you transform six squares of flat paper into a 3-D cube? **Find out with this amazing puzzle cube. Once you learn how to fold the first piece, it's easy to fold five more. The challenge is in fitting the folded pieces together.**

Step 1: Fold a square of paper in half. Crease and open.

Step 2: Fold the right side in to meet the center crease. Repeat on the left side.

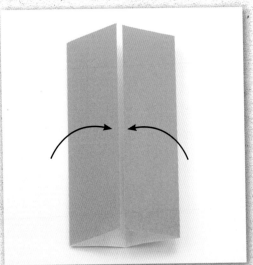

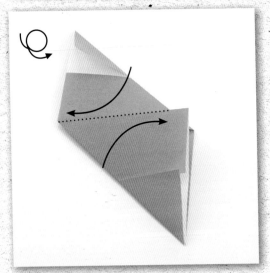

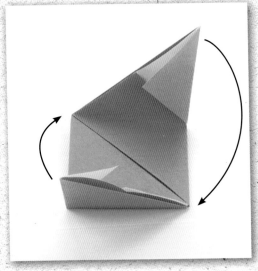

Step 3: Turn the paper over. Fold the lower left corner up to meet the right edge. Fold the upper right corner down to meet the left edge.

Step 4: Turn the model 90 degrees clockwise. Fold the top triangle down and the bottom triangle up to form a square. Crease all the folds well and let go. The piece will have a square in the middle with triangles standing up on the top and bottom.

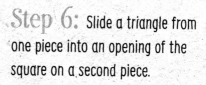

Step 5: Repeat steps 1-4 to make 6 pieces in different colors.

Step 6: Slide a triangle from one piece into an opening of the square on a second piece.

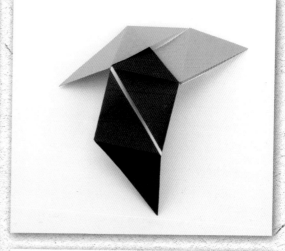

Step 7: Slide a triangle from a third piece into the opposite opening in the square of the first piece.

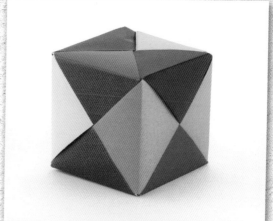

Step 8: Keep adding pieces onto each other until you have a colorful cube.

Tip: Make the pieces for another cube for a friend. Give him the pieces and a finished cube. Then see if he can figure out how to make the pieces fit together.

Jolly Roger Pirate Balloon

Who says that pirates sail only in ships? This Jolly Roger balloon warns others that tough sky pirates are on their way. Prepare to defend yourself, mateys!

MATERIALS

- 1 large balloon
- newspaper
- plain paper
- white glue
- water
- painting tray
- flexible wire, 12 inches (30.5 cm) long
- string
- black and white acrylic paint
- small paper cup
- plastic bowl

Step 1: Blow up the balloon and tie the end. Tear newspaper and plain paper into 2- by 2-inch (5- by 5-cm) squares. Make enough squares to cover the balloon three times.

Step 2: Mix ½ cup (120 milliliters) of white glue with ¼ cup (60 ml) of water in a plastic bowl. Pour enough into the painting tray to cover the bottom.

Step 3: Dip a newspaper square into the glue mixture and get it completely wet. Squeeze the paper between two fingers to wipe off the excess glue. Stick the paper to the balloon. Repeat this step to cover the balloon with paper squares. Overlap each square a bit so you can't see the surface of the balloon.

Step 4: Repeat step 3 with plain paper squares to cover the balloon with a second layer. Using plain paper will help you see the difference between the first and second layers.

Step 5: Repeat step 3 to make a third layer using newspaper squares.

97

Step 6: Tie the knotted end of the balloon to a piece of string. Hang the balloon up and allow it to dry completely. This will take 2 to 3 days.

Step 7: After the paper is dry, pull the knotted end of the balloon away from the dried paper. Pop the balloon with a pin. Pull out the balloon pieces and throw them away.

Step 8: Trim the opening at the base of the balloon to make a 2- to 3-inch (5- to 7.6-cm) wide hole. Use a hole punch to make four evenly spaced holes around the edge of the opening.

Step 9: Use a sharp pencil to make a small hole in the top of the balloon. Make a small loop in the end of the wire. Thread the wire through the hole from the inside of the balloon. The small loop will help hold the wire in place. Make a large loop in the wire on the outside to use for hanging the balloon.

Step 10: Paint the balloon with black paint. When it's dry, add a skull and crossbones on the front with white paint.

Step 11: Punch four holes around the top of the paper cup. Paint the paper cup to look like a basket.

Step 12: To attach the basket, tie four pieces of string between the holes in the cup and the balloon. Now your pirates are ready to launch!

Tip: If you don't like pirates, you can paint the balloon in other ways. Try painting one with a flag or the logo of your favorite sports team.

Hopping Paper Frogs

Did you know a flat piece of paper could become a hopping frog? It's easy to do, and any paper you have will work. Once this frog is folded, just push down on its backside to make it take a leap.

MATERIALS

- 6- by 6-inch (15- by 15-cm) squares of green paper
- marker

Tip: Use different sizes and colors of paper to make an army of hopping frogs. Have frog races with your friends.

Step 1: Fold the paper in half corner to corner to make a triangle pointing up.

Step 2: Fold the lower left corner up to the top point. Repeat with the lower right corner to form a diamond shape.

Step 3: Fold the left point of the diamond to the center. Repeat for the right and bottom points. The paper will now look like an open envelope.

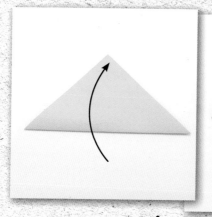

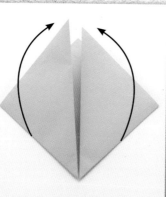

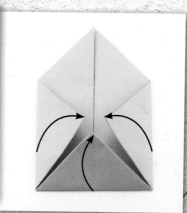

Step 4: Fold the left top flap to the left. It will overlap the left upper edge of the envelope. Repeat with the right top flap on the right side.

Step 5: Fold the bottom of the envelope up at the point where the seams meet. Then fold the top half of this new flap down to meet the bottom edge.

Step 6: Turn the model over. Draw eyes on the frog with a marker. To make the frog hop, press down on the back end until it flips away from your finger.

101

Terrific Indian Tepee

Have you ever wanted to travel back in time and see how American Indian tribes lived? This project can bring a little piece of that history into your own room. Find a grocery bag and some straight sticks to create this cool American Indian tepee.

MATERIALS

- pizza pan or round tray, 24 inches (61 cm) wide
- 1 large brown paper bag
- 4 dowels, 0.25 by 12 inches (0.6 by 30.5 cm)
- markers
- heavy brown string
- clear tape

Step 1: Use the four dowels to make the tepee frame. Place them together in an upside-down cone shape. Tie the tops of the dowels together with string.

Step 2: Cut down the length of one corner of a paper bag. Cut the bottom out of the bag. You will have one long, flat sheet of paper.

Step 3: Lay the pizza pan so half of it covers the paper. Trace along the outside edge of the pan to make a half circle on the paper. Remove the pan and cut out the half circle. It should be about 12 inches (30.5 cm) wide and 24 inches (61 cm) long.

Step 4: Wrap the paper around the tepee frame to see if it fits. There should be a 1-inch (2.5-cm) wide overlap where the ends meet. Trim away any excess paper.

Step 5: Lay the paper flat and decorate it with markers. Draw geometric shapes around the border. Use simple shapes to represent objects in nature such as the sun, stars, or various animals.

Step 6: Punch holes about 1 inch (2.5 cm) apart around the base of the tepee skin. Thread the string through the holes to form stitches. Tape the ends of the string to the inside of the paper.

Step 7: Fold the corners of the paper over the ends of the string and tape in place. Wrap the paper around the tepee frame and tape the overlap securely.

Tip: Make several tepees to create your own American Indian village.

Trihexaflexagon

Have fun turning a boring strip of paper into a magical 3-D gadget! **With a little creativity, you'll have a cool six-sided figure that can be flipped inside out to form different designs.**

MATERIALS
- strip of white printer paper, 1.5 by 11 inches (3.8 by 28 cm)
- markers or colored pencils

Step 1: Fold the left corner of the paper inward to form a small triangle. The folded side should be 1.75 inches (4.4 cm) long. Now fold the pointed corner up to form an equilateral triangle.

Step 2: Flip the paper over and fold a second equilateral triangle. Flip the paper again and fold a third triangle. Keep flipping and folding until you have 10 triangles. Open the strip and trim away the ends.

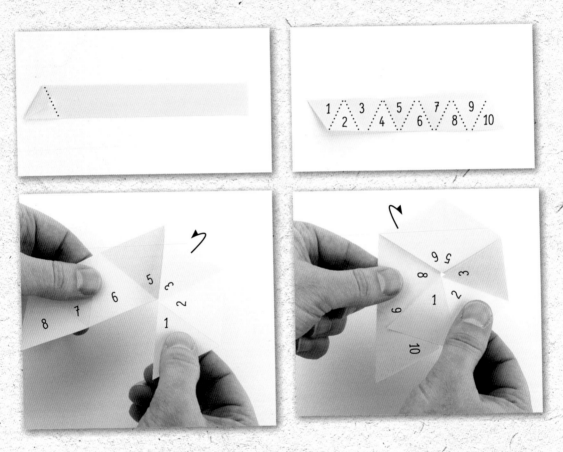

Step 3: Fold the fourth triangle behind the third.

Step 4: Fold the seventh triangle behind the sixth.

Tip: Be sure to flex the hexagon in both directions to see all six designs.

Step 5: Slip the first triangle behind the ninth.

Step 6: Turn the paper over. Then fold the tenth triangle under the first and glue it in place.

Step 7: Flex the flexagon by pinching the folds inward. Then open it again from the center.

Step 8: Decorate each of the three sides with markers or colored pencils. Now you're ready to impress your friends! Flip your flexagon inside out to show all the different designs.

107

Wild Rainforest Diorama

Get ready to go on an adventure! With this awesome 3-D diorama, you'll feel like you're on a real jungle safari. Listen carefully and you can almost hear the wildlife prowling around inside.

MATERIALS

- shoe box with a hinged lid
- small box, such as a tea box
- light and dark green acrylic paint
- cardstock paper
- nature magazines
- brown and green construction paper
- light and dark green tissue paper
- colored pencils or markers
- small twigs and rocks
- glue

Step 1: Open the shoe box and stand it on its end. Glue the small box between the back of the lid and the back side of the shoe box. The small box will help make the shoe box stable and keep the lid open.

Step 2: Paint the inside of the box. Use dark green at the bottom and light green at the top.

Step 3: Cut out one 7-inch (18-cm) wide rectangle of brown construction paper. Cut out two more 5-inch (13-cm) wide rectangles. Make all the rectangles 1 inch (2.5 cm) taller than the box. Draw a full tree on the large rectangle. Draw half trees on the smaller rectangles as shown. Give the trees a 0.5-inch (1.3-cm) wide tab along the sides and bottoms of the trunks. Cut out the trees and fold over the tabs.

Step 4: Place the trees by gluing the tabs to the inside edges of the box. Glue one half tree to the front of the lid. Glue the whole tree to the center of the box. Glue the other half tree inside the box near the back. Glue the tops of the branches to the ceiling of the box to hold them in place.

Step 5: Cut strips of tissue paper and crumple them to make leaves. Glue the tissue paper to the branches of the trees and the edges of the box. Add enough tissue paper to make it look like a rainforest.

Step 6: Cut ferns and other plants from green construction paper and glue them to the forest floor.

Step 7: Draw and color rainforest animals on cardstock and cut them out. Or glue photos of animals from nature magazines to cardstock and cut them out. Include animals such as crocodiles, gorillas, toucans, tigers, and snakes.

Step 8: Glue the animals to the trees, the leaves, the floor, and the top of the diorama.

Step 9: Add twigs and small rocks to complete your rainforest scene.

111

Build Fantastic Recycled Projects!

Think about everything you've thrown out recently. Maybe you threw away a milk jug, some newspapers, tin cans, or plastic water bottles. That may not seem like much, but people in the United States throw away nearly 251 million tons (228 million metric tons) of garbage every year!

Thankfully, all this trash can be greatly reduced by recycling. Many materials, such as glass, paper, plastic, and metals can be reused in new objects. For example, magazines and greeting cards can be made from recycled paper. Recycled plastic is often used to make new bottles and even furniture!

There are fun ways to recycle trash as well. Instead of throwing bottles and cans in the recycling bin, use them to make some awesome stuff! Get ready to build robots, UFOs, catapults, and other amazing projects while helping to keep Earth clean at the same time!

Balloon Badminton Set

Stuck inside on a rainy day? No problem! Just make a badminton set with stuff you have around the house. Then when the sun comes out you can use this set to play the game outside.

MATERIALS

- 1 pair of pantyhose
- 4 wire coat hangers
- duct tape
- 2 pieces of PVC pipe, 5 inches (13 cm) long
- small balloon
- roll of crepe paper

Step 1: Bend one wire hanger into a large oval shape. Bend the hook straight out to make the handle. Repeat this step with the other three hangers to make four wire frames.

Step 2: Place two wire frames together. Use small pieces of duct tape to attach them together. Space the tape about 1 inch (2.5 cm) apart. Repeat with the second pair of wire frames.

Step 3: Cut the legs off of the pair of pantyhose. Slip one leg piece over a wire frame. Wrap the excess end of the leg piece around the handle. Use a piece of duct tape to hold the material in place. Repeat this step for the second paddle.

Step 4: Place one paddle's handle into a piece of PVC pipe. Hot glue the pipe in place. Repeat for the second paddle.

Step 5: For indoor play, string a piece of crepe paper between two chairs for a net. Use the small balloon for a birdie.

Tip: If you don't have a real birdie for outdoor play, use a small sock rolled into a ball.

Creative Tin Can Lanterns

Don't throw out used tin cans. Wash them out and make some cool lanterns instead! These little lanterns can come in handy for a nighttime nature hike. Or you can use them as a decoration for your room.

MATERIALS

- several tin cans, 7 to 14 ounces (200 to 400 grams)
- black marker
- battery-operated tea light candles
- several pieces of stiff wire, 8 inches (20 cm) long
- acrylic paint (optional)

Step 1: Ask an adult to make sure the edges of your cans are smooth. Remove any labels from the cans and wash them well with soapy water. Dry the cans completely.

Step 2: Use a marker to make dots on the cans in the shape of footballs, skulls, bugs, or other objects. Mark an extra dot near the top on each side of the cans for the handles.

Step 3: Fill the cans with water and place them in the freezer until completely frozen.

Step 4: Ask an adult for help on this step. Fold a heavy towel on a sturdy work surface. Lay each can on its side. Use a hammer to tap the point of a nail through each dot to make holes.

117

Step 5: Place the cans in a big bowl of warm water to melt the ice. Dry off the cans and paint them if you wish.

Step 6: Use pliers to bend the ends of the wires into hook shapes. Bend the wires into large U shapes. Insert the hooked ends into the holes near the tops of the cans to form handles.

Step 7: Add battery-powered tea lights to each can. Now you're ready for a nighttime stroll at the nearest park!

Tip: Punch holes in the form of different constellations. Then place the can upside down over a tea light to project a starry night sky in your room.

Cool Coffee Can Birdhouse

Everyone needs a place to live, even the birds. With a recycled coffee can and some sticks, you can give homeless birds a warm, dry place to call home.

WELCOME HOME

MATERIALS

- 1 large plastic coffee container
- 1 sheet of plastic or a plastic placemat
- 1 plate, 12 inches (30.5 cm) wide
- many thin, straight sticks and twigs,
   4 to 7 inches (10 to 18 cm) long
- wood chips
- flexible wire, 3 feet (0.9 meter) long
- drill and drill bits

Step 1: Find an adult to help you before beginning this project. First clean the coffee container with soap and hot water. When dry, cut a 2.5- by 3-inch (6.4- by 7.6-cm) window in the can.

Step 2: Have an adult drill several small holes in the sides and bottom of the can. This helps keep moisture from building up inside the birdhouse. Drill a large hole under the center of the window. Insert a 4-inch (10-cm) long twig and hot glue it in place to make a perch.

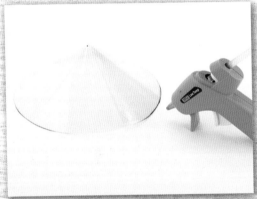

Step 3: Use the plate as a pattern to draw a circle on the plastic placemat. Cut out the circle. Mark the center point of the circle and cut a single line to that point. Overlap the two sides by 0.5 inch (1.3 cm) to form a cone. Glue the sides together.

Step 4: Twist a small loop onto one end of the wire. Thread the wire through the point of the cone. Hot glue the loop in place inside the cone. Glue the coffee can lid inside the cone. Cut off the excess plastic overlapping the lid.

Step 5: Use hot glue to cover the birdhouse with sticks and twigs. Glue them vertically, side by side. Measure and cut the sticks to fit over and under the window.

Step 6: Cover the roof with wood chips. Start at the outer edge and hot glue a row of chips. Glue the next row above so the chips overlap the first row about 0.5 inch (1.3 cm). Keep adding rows until the roof is covered. Twist the lid onto the coffee can to attach the roof.

Step 7: Hang the birdhouse from a tree by attaching the end of the wire to a branch.

Tip: Use the square piece of plastic that you cut out for the window to make a "Welcome Home" sign.

Rubber Band-Powered Car

Are you feeling the need for some speed? With a cardboard tube, some old CDs, and a few rubber bands, you can make this speedy race car. You'll be amazed at how far it can roll.

MATERIALS

- 8 identical water bottle caps
- 4 old CDs
- 5 to 10 rubber bands
- sturdy cardboard tube, such as an aluminum foil or waxed paper tube
- 2 sturdy plastic straws
- 2 bamboo skewers, 10 inches (25 cm) long
- stiff wire, 2 inches (5 cm) long
- acrylic paints

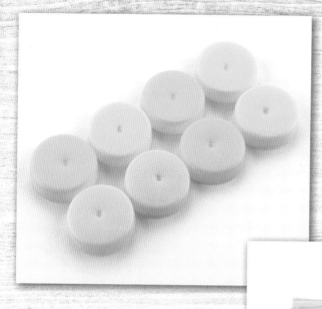

Step 1: Ask an adult to help you punch a hole in the center of each bottle cap. A sturdy nail works well for this. Make the holes just big enough to fit the bamboo skewer.

Step 2: Hot glue the bottle caps over the center holes of the CDs to make wheels. Glue one cap on each side of the CDs. Make sure the holes in the caps line up.

Step 3: Measure the width of the cardboard tube. Cut one piece of the plastic straw 2 inches (5 cm) longer than the width of the tube. Cut two more pieces of straw 1.5 inches (3.8 cm) long.

123

Step 4: Slide a bamboo skewer through one wheel, the long piece of straw, and a second wheel. Cut off the excess skewer next to the wheels. Repeat this step with two more wheels and the short straw pieces.

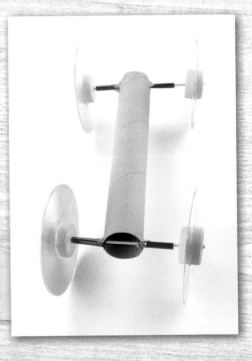

Step 5: Cut 0.5-inch (1.3-cm) long slits on opposite sides on one end of the cardboard tube. Widen the slits and push the axle with the long straw into the slits. Hot glue the straw piece in place.

Step 6: Repeat step 5 on the other end of the tube with the second axle. Be sure to leave a gap between the short straws inside the cardboard tube.

Tip: You can paint and decorate your car any way you wish. Try painting it to look like an IndyCar race car.

Step 7: Bend the 2-inch (5-cm) piece of wire into a small loop. Attach the wire loop to the center of the back axle. Glue the wire in place.

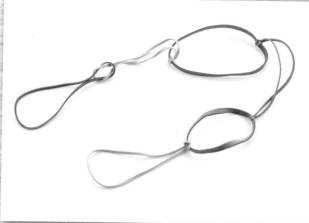

Step 8: Make a string of rubber bands by looping them together end to end.

Step 9: Tie or loop the end of the rubber band string around the front axle. Drop the string through the tube to the back end. Hook the other end of the rubber band string over the wire loop on the back axle. To make the car go, turn the back wheels to wind the rubber band around the axle. Then set down the car and watch it take off!

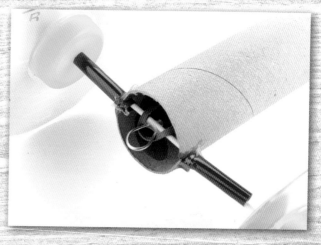

Plastic Bottle Mini Golf

Looking for a fun project on a slow summer day? Just wash out some plastic soda bottles and make your own mini golf course! Set them up in your backyard or at a local park, and then call your friends over for a game.

MATERIALS

- 9 plastic soda bottles, 3-liter size
- colorful duct tape
- permanent markers
- flat cardboard
- long cardboard tubes
- regular golf ball or lighter ball of similar size

Step 1: Ask an adult to help cut 2 inches (5 cm) off the bottom of each plastic bottle. Then cut a 3.5- by 4-inch (9- by 10-cm) arched door in the side of each bottle.

Step 2: Use duct tape to add a colorful stripe around the top of each bottle. Add large numbers to the stripes using permanent markers. Use markers to color a 1-inch (2.5-cm) border around the door openings. This will help make them easier to see from a distance.

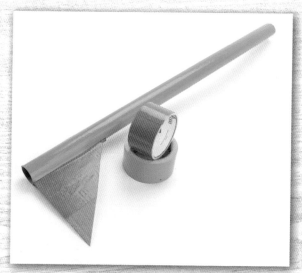

Step 3: For golf clubs, cut out a 6-inch (15-cm) wide triangle of cardboard. Cut a 6-inch (15-cm) long slit in one end of the cardboard tube. Slide the flat piece of cardboard into the slit and tape it in place. Wrap the whole club with colorful duct tape.

Step 4: Set up the golf course by pushing the soda bottles into the grass. Space them out to make the golf course a challenge.

Tip: Make your golf course even more challenging by adding obstacles. You can set up open cardboard boxes, cardboard containers, ramps, and large rocks.

Klink, the Robot Bank

Do you have some empty cans in the recycle bin? Grab them and turn them into this awesome android to guard your hard-earned cash!

MATERIALS

- 1 large coffee can with plastic lid, 40-ounce (1,130-gm) size
- 1 medium cardboard or plastic container with lid, 28-ounce (800-gm) size
- 2 small tin cans, 12-ounce (340-gm) size
- 2 toilet paper rolls
- silver acrylic paint
- markers
- colored duct tape
- large metal nuts, washers, gears, or other objects

Step 1: Place the medium can on the center of the lid of the large can. Trace a circle around the medium can onto the lid. Draw a second, smaller circle about 0.5 inch (1.3 cm) inside the first circle. Ask an adult to help cut out the smaller circle.

Step 2: Cut a coin-size slot in the medium can for a mouth.

Step 3: Paint all of the cans, lids, and cardboard tubes silver. Allow them to dry completely. Add stripes of colored duct tape to the base of the cardboard tubes and small cans.

Step 4: Hot glue the robot's body parts together. Glue the medium can to the top of the large can for the head. Glue the small cans to the bottom to make legs. Glue the cardboard tubes to the sides to make arms.

Step 5: Glue the metal nuts to the head to make eyes. Glue on more nuts, washers, and other objects to make a nose, ears, switches, or buttons.

Step 6: Your robot is ready to guard your treasure! Feed him by dropping quarters, dimes, nickels, and pennies into his mouth.

Hip Soda Tab Bracelet

Don't just toss those soda cans into the recycle bin. Pull off the tabs and save them to make this bracelet. Once you know how to make it, you'll want to make more of them for your friends.

MATERIALS
- colorful elastic cord
- tape
- about 25 soda can tabs

131

Step 1: Cut a piece of elastic cord 3 feet (0.9 m) long. Mark the middle with a piece of tape.

Step 2: Thread the ends of the elastic cord up through the openings in one tab. Pull the tab to the middle point of the cord. The cord should loop around the middle bar of the tab.

Step 3: Hold a second tab on top of tab one so the holes line up. The rough sides of the tabs should be back to back. Thread the cord over the left side of tab two and down through the holes of both tabs.

Step 4: Hold a third tab under tab two. Thread the cord under the right side of tab one and up through the holes in tab two. Then thread the cord over the right side of tab two and down through the holes in tab three.

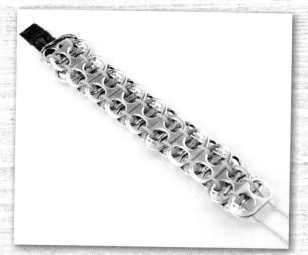

Step 5: Repeat step 4 with more tabs. Keep adding tabs until you have a string long enough to fit around your wrist. You will end up with two rows of side-by-side tabs with the smooth sides facing out.

Step 6: Remove the piece of tape from the elastic cord. Tie the ends of the cord to the sides of the first tab. Cut off any excess cord. Add a dab of hot glue to hold the knot in place.

Tip: You can make a matching necklace or even a belt using this same process. Just use a longer piece of elastic cord and more can tabs.

Eerie Glowing Alien Mask

All you need for an out-of-this-world mask is a single milk jug and a little glow-in-the-dark paint. Use it to scare your friends or hang it up in your bedroom for an eerie decoration.

MATERIALS

- 1-gallon (4-liter) milk jug
- marker
- green glow-in-the-dark paint
- elastic cord

Step 1: Ask an adult to help you cut the milk jug. First cut away the spout and surrounding top fourth of the jug.

Step 2: Cut a slit down the back along the curved edge. Continue cutting across one half of the bottom. Make another cut across the bottom perpendicular to the first cut. Fold the two sides toward the front.

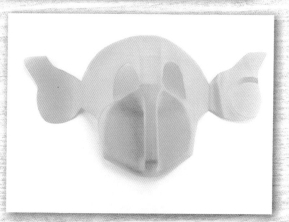

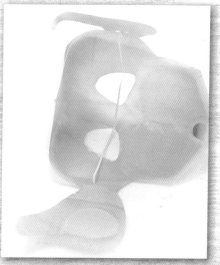

Step 3: Draw eyes just above the jug handle. Draw alien ears on the two side flaps. Ask an adult to help cut out the eyes and ears. Then paint your mask with glow-in-the-dark paint and let it dry completely.

Step 4: Punch holes in the sides of the mask. Tie a piece of elastic cord to the holes to hold the mask on your head. Now turn off the lights and get ready to freak out your friends!

135

Marshmallow Catapult

First raid the cupboard for a bag of marshmallows. Then launch some fun with this awesome catapult. Watch out for flying marshmallows!

MATERIALS

- 4 jumbo wooden craft sticks
- several heavy duty zip ties
- 1 0.75-inch (2-cm) heavy binder clip
- plastic spoon
- marshmallows

Step 1: Place two craft sticks together. Wrap a zip tie about 1 inch (2.5 cm) from the end.

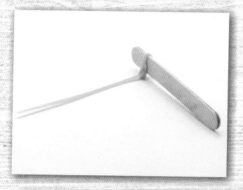

Step 2: Wedge one silver tab on the binder clip between the craft sticks. Slide a zip tie through the black base of the binder clip and wrap it around the craft sticks. Wrap a third zip tie around the craft sticks about 1.5 inches (3.8 cm) above the binder clip. Tighten all the zip ties and trim away the ends.

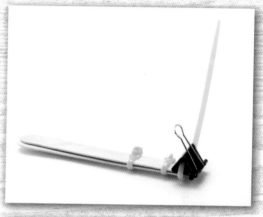

Step 3: Repeat steps 1 and 2 with two more craft sticks on the other side of the binder clip.

Step 4: Place the plastic spoon on top of the second set of craft sticks. Wrap and tighten two or three zip ties around the spoon to hold it in place. Tighten the ties and trim off the ends.

Step 5: To shoot a marshmallow, place the catapult on a flat surface and hold it down. Place a marshmallow on the spoon. Push the spoon down and release it to launch the marshmallow. Be careful not to pinch your fingers in the binder clip.

Awesome Glowing UFO

Is it a plane? Is it a meteor? No, it's a glowing UFO! Paper plates and silver paint are just right for making a mysterious alien craft. This spaceship could make a great prop for a homemade science fiction movie.

MATERIALS

- 4 plain white paper plates, 9 inches (23 cm) wide
- 1 clear bottle cap (found on toiletry bottles)
- 1 large paper cup
- 3 or 4 sturdy straws
- 1 pencil
- silver paint
- battery-operated tea light candle

Step 1: Glue two paper plates together. When dry, flip them upside down and mark the back into eight equal sections. Trace around the bottle cap to make a circle at the center where the lines intersect.

Step 2: Cut along the lines inside the circle. Push the open end of the bottle cap through the hole so the top part sticks out about 1 inch (2.5 cm).

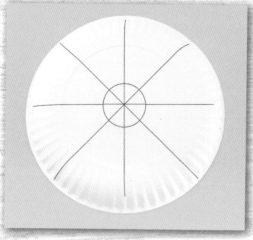

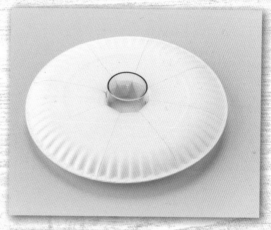

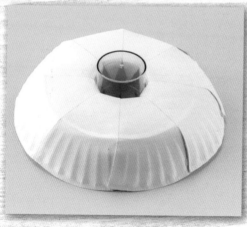

Step 3: Flip the plate again and cut along the marks from the outer edge to the inner plate rim. Overlap the cut sections by about 0.25 inch (0.6 cm) and hot glue them in place. The plate will now be shaped like an upside down bowl.

Step 4: Glue two more paper plates together. Place the paper cup upside down on the center of the plate. Trace a circle around the cup. Mark the circle into eight equal sections. Cut along the marks, stopping 0.25 inch (0.6 cm) from the edge of the circle.

Step 5: Open up the flaps and push the bottom of the paper cup through the hole. It should stick out about 1.5 inches (3.8 cm). Glue the flaps to the cup to hold it in place.

Step 6: Place the dome section over the bottom plate. Measure the distance between the two sections. Remove the bottom section and cut slits in the top of the cup equal to the distance measured. Bend the flaps out.

Step 7: Cut slits for windows in the bottom part of the paper cup. Cut out larger windows and portholes in the dome section.

Step 8: Cut three to four small X's in the bottom section for the straws. Push the straws through the holes. Glue them in place at an angle to make the UFO's landing gear.

Step 9: Cut several slits along the edge of the bottom section. Fold the flaps up, overlap them, and glue them to form a bowl shape. Insert the bottom section into the dome section. Hot glue the dome to the bottom section and the paper cup flaps to hold everything in place.

Step 10: Paint everything silver and allow the UFO to dry.

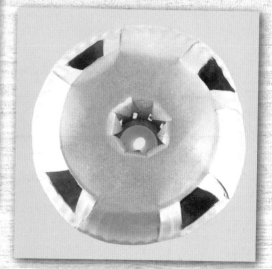

Step 11: Turn on the battery tea light and place it at the bottom of the paper cup. Then replace the clear dome. Your UFO should be lit up and ready to decorate your room!

Tip: Try adding extra straws to make blaster guns or toilet paper tubes for engines. You can also try using glow-in-the-dark paint instead of silver paint.

Soda Bottle Mudguard

If you like riding your bike through puddles then you'll like this quick and easy project. Use a plastic soda bottle and a cable tie to help keep you clean when riding through the mud.

MATERIALS
- markers
- 1 plastic soda bottle with cap, 2-liter size
- large plastic cable tie
- acrylic paint

Step 1: Make two marks on the bottle cap the same width as the plastic cable tie. Ask an adult to help cut slits into the cap at the marks. Thread the cable tie in and out of the slits.

Step 2: Wrap the cable tie around the seat post of your bike. Or wrap it around the bike frame just above the rear wheel. Be sure the bottle cap points toward the back wheel of the bike.

Step 3: Ask an adult to help you cut off the bottom of the soda bottle at an angle. Screw the bottle snugly onto the bottle cap. Then mark out a curved mudguard shape on the bottle. Remove the bottle and cut it along the marks. Be sure to leave the top of the bottle intact so it can be screwed back onto the bottle cap.

Step 4: Snugly screw the bottle back onto the cap to complete your mudguard. You're ready to ride!

Tip: Cover the mudguard with acrylic paint and allow to dry completely. Then use permanent markers to add flames or lightning bolts.

Capstone Press is published by Capstone,
1710 Roe Crest Drive, North Mankato, Minnesota 56003
www.capstonepub.com

Library of Congress Cataloging-in-Publication Data
Ventura, Marne, author.
Big book of building : duct tape, paper, cardboard, and recycled projects to blast
away boredom / by Marne Ventura.
pages cm
Audience: 8–12.
Audience: 4–6.
Summary: "Simple step-by-step instructions teach readers how to make original
projects from duct tape, paper, cardboard, and recyclable materials"—Provided
by publisher.
ISBN 978-1-4914-4371-2 (paperback)
ISBN 978-1-4914-7597-3 (eBook PDF)
ISBN 978-1-4914-7892-9 (ePub)
1. Handicraft—Juvenile literature. 2. Refuse as art material—Juvenile literature.
3. Recycled products—Juvenile literature. I. Title.
TT160.V44835 2016
745.5—dc23   2015001426

Editorial Credits
Aaron Sautter, editor; Richard Korab and Katy LaVigne, designers;
Ted Williams, art director; Sarah Schuette, studio stylist; Marcy Morin,
studio scheduler; Gene Bentdahl, production specialist

Photo Credits
All photographs by Capstone Studio: Karon Dubke

Design Elements
iStockphoto: studio9400
Shutterstock: Alhovik, Asya Alexandrova, Carsten Reisinger, donates 1205,
happydancing, Irina Tischenko, kao, Luminis, M.E. Mulder, nayneung1, Roman
Samokhin, Ronald Sumners, R-studio, Sharon Day, slava17, stuart.ford

Printed in China.
062015   008868RRDF15